MICROCOSM PUBLISHING is Portland's most diversified publishing house and distributor with a focus on the colorful, authentic, and empowering. Our books and zines have put your power in your hands since 1996, equipping readers to make positive changes in their lives and in the world around them. Microcosm emphasizes skill-building, showing hidden histories, and fostering creativity through challenging conventional publishing wisdom with books and bookettes about DIY skills, food, bicycling, gender, self-care, and social justice. What was once a distro and record label started by Joe Biel in a drafty bedroom was determined to be *Publishers Weekly*'s fastest-growing publisher of 2022 and has become among the oldest independent publishing houses in Portland, OR, and Cleveland, OH. We are a politically moderate, centrist publisher in a world that has inched to the right for the past 80 years.

TABLE OF CONTENTS

INTRODUCTION

*D*o bookstores even need to be protected? I can easily imagine some bookstore owners or workers saying no. After all, a bookstore, a for-profit business, doesn't need protection in the same way that, say, civil rights do. Civil rights are under attack, and have been for decades. I have no qualms about saying civil rights need to be protected. Bookstores, though? Maybe it's a more complicated story. A business has to figure out how to make money to stay open, so if a bookstore fails, that's a business problem, not a cultural problem. Right? On top of that, lots of bookstores aren't failing at all. By many indicators, the number of bookstores in America is increasing. Some people have even suggested that America is in the midst of an indie bookstore renaissance. If that's the case, why worry about protecting bookstores?

First off, I want to make it clear that a bookstore is not a charity and should not be treated as such. As much as folks in my field may argue differently, there is nothing inherently godlike in the act of putting a ton of books into a room and asking people to give you money so they can take them home. Important, sure. Noble? No. The problem with "noble" versus "important" is that casting an air of holiness over the work of selling books makes it too easy to exploit the people doing that work. More on that later.

So, given that bookstores aren't noble charities, what's the argument for protecting them? The fact is, despite some data indicating that things are pretty good for bookstores right now, there remain many reasons why they need to be protected. For one thing, the current "indie bookstore renaissance," if you want to call it that, is being driven by a historically diverse class of new booksellers and bookstore owners. In a July 2022 *New York Times* article, journalists Alexandra Alter and Elizabeth A. Harris claim that "the book selling business—traditionally overwhelmingly white—has . . . become much more diverse" because "many of the new stores that opened during the pandemic are run by nonwhite booksellers."[1] Stores from New York City (Yu and Me Books) to Los Angeles (the Salt Eaters Bookshop) and from St. Paul (Black Garnet Books) to St. Louis (the Noir Bookshop) have opened in the past few years under the leadership of new booksellers from marginalized backgrounds. In an email, American Booksellers Association CEO Allison Hill told me that since January 2020, 96 new bookstores have been opened by self-identified people of color. This diversification of booksellers is great news, especially considering the obstacles that kept

1 Alexandra Alter and Elizabeth A. Harris, "Some Surprising Good News: Bookstores Are Booming and Becoming More Diverse," *New York Times,* July 10, 2022, https://www.nytimes.com/2022/07/10/books/bookstores-diversity-pandemic.html.

bookselling so white in the first place. Opening a bookstore is staggeringly expensive—a new bookstore owner can spend hundreds of thousands of dollars in buildout, staffing, and initial inventory costs before a single book is sold. People of color, queer people, and other marginalized groups have generally had a much harder time accessing that kind of capital. Therefore, most of the folks who have historically opened bookstores have come from backgrounds (read: white, upper and upper-middle class) that give them more access to capital and generational wealth. The fact that a new generation of booksellers is creative and persistent enough to work around this issue does not mean the issue is gone. And then there's this: opening a bookstore is a major challenge; but keeping it open is another. According to Gary Rivlin's book *Saving Main Street*, "One in three small businesses in the United States close before celebrating a second anniversary." Further, "Seventy percent are dead within a decade."[2] Because this exciting, diverse new generation of booksellers has overcome the once-insurmountable challenge of opening a store, and because they face a new set of major challenges, bookstores need to be protected.

Working in books is also growing more dangerous, especially for members of these marginalized groups. Somewhat unwittingly, bookstores and libraries (and the workers who make them tick) have ended up in the middle of a violent and ruthless culture war. Radical right-wingers, including some at the very peak of influence within the national Republican Party, have seized onto books as a battleground.[3] They primarily target children's books by queer authors and authors of color to force their regressive political vision onto America. The bookstores and libraries that disseminate these materials are therefore targets. Social media campaigns, verbal harassment, threatening phone calls, disruptive protests, and other social and political weapons are pointed at people who are doing the simple work of helping marginalized readers see themselves in books. Hundreds of Drag Queen Story Hours have been disrupted by protestors spouting hate speech. A bookstore in Oklahoma faced harassment for making tee shirts with a QR code linking to a list of banned books. Personally, I received threats over Twitter for defending a fellow bookseller's right to free speech. As part of this online harassment campaign, people began ordering *Mein Kampf* from my store. As a bookseller, particularly a leftist Jewish bookseller, even writing this feels a little frightening to me. And for good reason: In November 2022, the Jewish-owned Iliad Bookshop in Los Angeles was the target of an

2 Gary Rivlin, *Saving Main Street* (New York: HarperCollins, 2022), 10.
3 Brendan Farrington, "DeSantis Signs Bill Targeting Explicit Books in Schools," *Associated Press*, March 25, 2022, https://apnews.com/article/entertainment-florida-ron-desantis-school-boards-libraries-da50c9c4091868e121484425d290385b.

arson attack, with rambling conspiracy-theory flyers left at the scene. Recently, Gretchen Treu, co-owner of A Room of One's Own Bookstore in Madison, Wisconsin, told me, "At one of our recent staff meetings, we were talking about what [happens] when someone comes in with a gun, because we're going to be a target. We're openly progressive, openly queer, openly trans, and that's getting scarier and scarier." Notice that Gretchen didn't say *if* someone comes in with a gun. Bookstores need to be protected.

Even as bookselling work becomes increasingly dangerous, it's also increasingly valuable to communities. Any independently owned retail business provides benefits to its community. A central district with several thriving small businesses is an economic boon to any city. Such concentration of small businesses draws tourists, locals, and workers who spend and earn money that's more likely to stay local. According to a 2022 report by the American Booksellers Association, "Independent businesses provide [their] communities with substantial, quantifiable economic benefits relative to their chain competitors" as they "distribute profits to local ownership, employ a variety of personnel that might otherwise reside at a distant corporate office, routinely purchase goods and services from other local businesses, and generously support local charitable causes."[4] To quantify these benefits, the report claims that "Approximately 29% of all revenue at independent bookstores immediately recirculates in the local economy. This translates to a local impact advantage of 109% that of chain competitor Barnes & Noble, and a massive 405% local impact advantage over Amazon."[5] It's easy to invoke the emotional or cultural reasons that small businesses should be allowed to thrive; equally important is the clear data that shows bookstores and other small businesses are good for their communities in an economic sense, too.

Even more so than other locally owned small businesses, bookstores can lead the charge in generating sustainable economic activity for a city or community. According to a major report by the UK's Institute of Place Management, bookstores in particular "significantly contribute to the vitality and viability of their high streets."[6] They do this in myriad ways, from hosting events to providing jobs to helping surprise readers with new material. Many of these will be explored in the pages to come. But, crucially, bookstores have a way of lifting up other Main Street businesses: the Institute of Place Management

4 American Booksellers Association and Civic Economics, *Unfulfilled: Amazon and the American Retail Landscape* (2022), 4.
5 ABA and Civic Economics, *Unfulfilled*, 4.
6 Chris Gregory, Regine Sonderland Saga, and Cathy Parker. *Booksellers as Placemakers: The Contribution of Booksellers to the Vitality and Viability of High Streets* (Institute of Place Management, 2022).

claims, "The presence of bookshops can be expected to support wider high street activity, helping to prevent urban decay, increase or maintain property values and provide footfall for neighbouring businesses."[7] On top of all that, in the words of journalist Gary Rivlin, small businesses are "central to people's perception of what it [means] to live in a place."[8] A town's unique character is built by its small businesses. Because of the positive ripple effects a bookstore can have in its community, bookstores need to be protected.

However, while towns feel the economic benefits of bookstores, too often booksellers themselves do not. Bookselling has a reputation as a difficult and low-paying job, for good reason. Retail work in general means a lot of contact with an often-unruly public, long hours on your feet, impossible customer demands, and physically grueling job duties. Benefits are few and far between, and they're often invisible. Rather than, say, PTO and health insurance, booksellers are often told that the perks of their job are advance copies of books and the opportunity to meet authors. The industry can get away with treating workers like this because bookselling is so often treated as a calling. Of course I believe bookstores do important work, and I wrote extensively about why exactly that's true in my book *How to Resist Amazon and Why*. The work is important. But so is protecting the workers who do it. Labor writer Kim Kelly writes, "It is an awful secret that so many of the workers who bring these cherished [books] to life are struggling with low wages, racial and gender inequities, and unsafe working conditions."[9]

Often, bookstore owners and managers point to the business's tight margins as a reason that higher compensation and benefits aren't possible. I see their point. Bookselling as it exists is an industry of scarcity. When discussing this issue with me, novelist and bookstore owner Louise Erdrich told me, "We're now contented with the crumbs of what it was." Corporate greed and consolidation are driving this crisis. You better believe top executives at behemoth publishers have wonderful pay and benefits, even as they offer cost-of-living raises that fall far behind inflation. Even as they bust up any unionizing efforts. These publishers tout record profits, even as bookstores can't make enough to properly pay their employees. At an even larger scale, Amazon, the country's biggest retailer of books, is in the midst of a decades-long campaign to make people think books are worth less than they actually are, which ultimately leads to less money flowing into the system. And less money flowing into the system means less money reaching those at the bottom (but again, of course, the people at the top are always going to be fine).

7 Gregory, Sonderland Saga, and Parker, *Booksellers as Placemakers*, 7.
8 Rivlin, *Saving Main Street*, 14.
9 Kim Kelly, "Bookstore Workers Are Forming Unions Over Low Pay and Lack of Benefits," *Teen Vogue*, May 5, 2022, https://www.teenvogue.com/story/bookstore-workers-union.

I don't want to protect bad bosses or unsustainable, underpaid bookselling jobs. I *do* want to protect the vibrancy of bookselling in general. Paying booksellers too little is not the answer. Answering scarcity with scarcity will do nothing except create a race to zero. The mindset that we can scrimp and cut and whittle our way to a thriving bookstore industry is not sustainable. Trying to thrive by holding our breath will only find bookstores bouncing from crisis to crisis. We—readers, booksellers, publishers, bookstore fans—must find ways to make bookselling a sustainable career. Only then will bookstores find a bright future. That's why this zine advocates for labor unions, higher minimum wages, alternative bookstore models, and other worker-friendly measures: the future of bookstores is booksellers, and they need to be protected.

One vital role those booksellers can play is to introduce readers to new books, authors, and even social movements. There's a rich history of radical, activist, and feminist bookstores that serve as a durable entry point into social movements for burgeoning activists. In this way, a bookstore is actually more than a bookstore. As Kimberly Kinder writes in her book *The Radical Bookstore: Counter-Space for Social Movements*, "Activists operating bookstores and infoshops rarely maintain single-use storefronts. Instead, they treat the space as an enabling resource sustaining many functions through continual repurposing."[10] Selling books is a function of these bookstores, yes, but so are lots of other things. A crucial element of bookstores is permanence: while a protest can last a few hours, a radical bookstore can last decades. Kinder calls radical bookstores "constructed spaces that find a home in retail and that leverage the durability and porosity of retail to advance political causes"; as she writes, "Having autonomous space, instead of relying only on seized or borrowed space, constructs additional opportunities for organizing."[11] Because bookstores are permanent or semi-permanent spaces, activists can easily use them to advance their causes and welcome new activists into the fold. Viewed in this context, the bookstore is no longer simply a cute place to buy books; it's an incubator for activists and changemakers. As Kinder explains, "The point of constructing radical bookstores and libraries is not to make quaint community spaces. On the contrary, the point is to challenge capitalism, imperialism, white privilege, patriarchy, and homophobia in a significant way that poses material threats to existing systems of power."[12] Put simply, a radical bookstore has the capacity to change the world. Let's protect these spaces so they can do their work.

10 Kimberly Kinder, *The Radical Bookstore: Counter-Space for Social Movements* (Minneapolis: University of Minnesota Press, 2021), 6.
11 Kinder, *Radical Bookstore*, 3.
12 Kinder, *Radical Bookstore*, 4.

Finally, while I reiterate that bookselling is not inherently sacred, books can certainly be important. Though they're not charities, bookstores are doing significant cultural work. My good friend Jeff Deutsch, director of Chicago's Seminary Co-op Bookstores, has long spoken eloquently and passionately about the cultural value of what he calls "good bookstores." In his 2022 book, *In Praise of Good Bookstores*, Deutsch writes that "good bookstores are a repository for great books and a testing ground for recently published aspirants to greatness."[13] Here is the most bookish reason to protect bookstores: they are powerful machines for uplifting, celebrating, discovering, and ultimately selling good books. In doing this work, Deutsch claims, booksellers are "providing great cultural labor, these transcendental readers, these professors of books."[14] It can be argued that this is the most important job of the bookseller: to find and promote and love the books that are good, that do good in this world. The groundbreaking books, the books that tell important stories, the books that see and elevate historically marginalized people. Amazon doesn't care about this work; they see books as mere objects in their massive data-collecting flywheel machine. This is also increasingly true of the so-called "Big Five" publishers: Penguin Random House, HarperCollins, Hachette, Macmillan, and Simon & Schuster. These publishers, the biggest makers and sellers of books in the world, have increasingly given their attention to blockbusters. If the biggest makers and sellers of books are focusing on books that will simply make the most money, who is left to advocate for the offbeat, the groundbreaking, the dare-I-say *important*? Booksellers. Bookstores. Bookstores are crucial in creating a world of books beyond those that appear on Walmart's shelves; for this reason, bookstores should be protected.

What follows is a list of 50 ways to protect bookstores. It's not a checklist, and I wouldn't expect anyone to try to do all 50. Plus, some of them are quite specifically aimed at politicians or publishers or shitty landlords. While I recognize that few readers of this zine will actually be shitty landlords, maybe you know a shitty landlord and you can use what you learn here to gently nudge your landlord friend to be a bit less shitty. Similarly, even if you're not a politician, you can always hop on the phone to your representative's office and talk to them about the stuff in this zine, and I highly encourage you to do so.

Perhaps the seasoned reader of nonfiction about bookstores might have noticed that I'm not using the term "independent bookstores" or "indie bookstores." That is a conscious choice. It's hard to trace the origin of the term "independent bookstore," but Dan Cullen, former senior strategy officer for the American Booksellers Association, tells me he's pretty sure it was invented

---

13 Jeff Deutsch, *In Praise of Good Bookstores* (Princeton: Princeton University Press, 2022), 79.
14 Deutsch, *Good Bookstores*, 90.

as a way to distinguish small, locally owned bookstores from national chains like Borders, Barnes & Noble, and B. Dalton. I worry that when I say "indie bookstore," the reader will imagine one specific kind of place—maybe a tiny store. A store on a main street in a downtown row of storefronts. A quiet store. A store operated by a single owner. I even fear some people might make assumptions about what type of person becomes an "independent bookstore owner"—assumptions about age, race, and class. "Bookstore," being a broader term with fewer cultural assumptions associated with it, is useful in this project that seeks to broaden the idea of what bookstores can do. Additionally, given the demise of so many chain megastores and the rise of Amazon, I'm not sure the "indie" versus "not indie" distinction is quite so important anymore (more on that later). Of course, there are benefits to supporting locally owned small businesses instead of national chains, and I'll discuss those in detail in the pages to come. Still, the fight to protect bookstores has taken on a different tenor in the decades since "independent bookstore" came into use.

Ultimately, my goal with this zine is pretty simple: help create the conditions that will enable a world where bookstores and booksellers can thrive. Maybe you agree, and in that case, read on for ways you can help bookstores have a bright and vibrant future in which they continue to do important cultural work. Even better, let's create a world where the people doing that important work can be properly compensated, celebrated, and rewarded for their efforts.

I. INDIVIDUAL HABITS AND CHOICES

*M*any of the issues facing bookstores are systemic, and I never want to leave it up to individual choices to solve systemic problems. That's why suggestions involving things like individual shopping habits, social media usage, and lifestyle choices only make up part of this zine; later on, there are also suggestions for policy changes and community action. Still, there are lots of things individuals can do in their daily lives to help bookstores in general, and their local bookstores in particular. Here are several of them.

1. Buy books in person at bookstores

The best, easiest, and most fun way to protect a bookstore is to make a habit of buying books there. While many bookstores have adapted to a more online world, I'd argue that there's still no match for the experience of browsing in a bookstore. A good bookstore is a complex organism designed to slow you down and connect you with books, and the best ones do that trick very well. Jeff Deutsch writes that "the good bookstore sells books, but its primary product, if you will, is the browsing experience."[15] A well-designed bookstore space is something magical, a space that works to force you to slow down. A bookstore can create an elusive quiet, a surprising peace that even I, lifelong habitant of bookstores, still find myself chasing. On the experience of browsing a bookstore, Jason Guriel writes, "How wonderfully subversive it was to feel like I was alone in a city."[16]

In regards to protecting bookstores, though, buying books in person just makes the most sense for the bookstore. In high-minded terms, it's what the stores are designed to do. In practical terms, it makes the most economic sense. In-person buying bypasses the expense of shipping materials and the extra employee time it takes to process an online order. For another thing, it's fun for us. We like it. The positive customer interactions are what keep us going even when working in retail gets difficult. Selling books to you in our building is what we're set up to do, and doing it a lot will protect our futures.

I'll pause here to note that I understand that buying new books isn't an economic possibility for everyone. This is especially true as the price of books goes up due to paper shortages, supply chain challenges, and, you guessed it, corporate greed. As an answer, I'll voice my support of used bookstores as well. A used bookstore brings many of the same benefits to a community as

---

15 Deutsch, *Good Bookstores*, 24.
16 Jason Guriel, "I Remember the Bookstore," *Longreads*, November 10, 2022, longreads.com/2022/11/10/i-remember-the-bookstore/.

a store that sells new books, with the added bonus that the books are more affordable. Additionally, buying used books is one way to allay concerns about the environmental impact of printing new books. And of course, I don't want the only answer to be "spend money." With that in mind, of the 50 items on this list, at least 31 are things you can do or advocate for without spending a dime. While selling books is of course our bread and butter, and the people buying books are a necessary component of that, it's far from the only way to protect bookstores.

2. Buy books from locally owned bookstores

People ask me all the time what I think about Barnes & Noble. It's a complicated question to answer. Many booksellers working today still remember the big chains as the enemy, sometimes literally: at one point in the 1990s, the American Booksellers Association sued Barnes & Noble and Borders for price-fixing schemes. With the continued widespread use of the term "independent bookstore," the idea that chains are bad is baked into the identity of many American bookstores.

Still, there's one big difference between now and the era that spawned "independent bookstores": Amazon. Amazon's control of the book market is already vast and near total. The disappearance of chain bookstores would only increase that power; indeed, the very act of selling books to browsers in a building dedicated to that purpose is at risk thanks to Jeff Bezos and company, regardless of whether that building is a tiny historic storefront or a boxy anchor in a suburban strip mall. I'd be remiss in not saying that.

However, the point remains, there are tremendous economic, community, and cultural benefits to buying books from locally owned bookstores, many of which are outlined in the rest of this zine. Buying books in person from a store dedicated to books is a good thing; if that store is owned by members of your community, even better.

3. Buy books from bookstores online

If buying books in person from a bookstore isn't feasible—say, your town doesn't have a bookstore, or circumstances don't allow you to regularly visit a store—buying a book online is the next best choice. Nearly all bookstores have an online-buying option, and many of them sell books directly through their website (this is what we do at the bookstore where I work, the Raven). Buying books online directly from a bookstore as opposed to, say, Bookshop.org (see item #10 on this list) gives the bookstore a bigger cut of the book's price. When you buy a book in store, the store gets 40–46% of the sticker price. When you buy online, the store gets the same cut, but subtract the cost of shipping materials and the extra labor it takes to process an online order. Processing an online order is a complicated task, and often what stores charge for shipping and handling doesn't cover it all. (For further discussion of shipping and handling costs, see #29 on this list.) Other online options like Libro.fm and Bookshop.org, while helpful, give bookstores a smaller cut of the cost of a book. So, ultimately, if you can't make it to a store for whatever reason, and you're still able to purchase books, grab those books via a store's website.

4. Buy non-book stuff from bookstores

It's a bit of a painful irony, but books aren't the most profitable things we sell. Yes, our bread and butter doesn't make us a ton of money. As previously stated, a bookstore keeps 40–46% of the price of a book. If a book were to cost $5, that means a bookstore would keep around $2.30. Compared to other retail goods, this is actually a low markup. A movie theater, for instance, can keep up to $4.63 from the sale of a $5 bag of popcorn.[17] The reasons for the low markups on books are numerous and complicated, but they shake down to the perceived value of books, combined with the fact that nearly all books come with the price printed on them. (For further explanation on why book markups are so low, refer to #31 on this list.) This low-markup issue in books is one of the factors that leads bookstores to sell other things, like stationery, greeting cards, and notebooks. These not only have better wholesale pricing than books; they also don't come pre-printed with the price, unlike books. All this means that bookstores generally make a bit more money on non-book stuff than they do on books themselves.

5. Buy bookstore merch from bookstores

Many bookstores offer merchandise featuring their name and branding. If you read item #4 on this list, you already know one of the reasons why bookstores do this: we can set our own margins on merch we create. Here's another good reason to buy and wear bookstore merch: you're helping the bookstore build recognition. You may even meet a fellow fan of the store. Every time you go out in public or post a picture of yourself wearing a bookstore shirt, you're helping that bookstore a little bit.

6. Buy books for your work, club, or group from bookstores

Plenty of organizations give away books in large quantities: political campaigns, corporations, libraries, schools, you name it. I'd argue that bookstores are not only *a* place to coordinate these bulk buys; they are the *best* place to do it. By placing a big bulk order through a bookstore, you're going to get personalized

---

17 Diane Dragan, "10 Outrageous Markups You'd Never Guess You Were Paying," RD.com, March 16, 2022, rd.com/list/10-outrageous-markups-youd-never-guess-you-were-paying/.

attention from a bookseller who's going to make sure everything goes smoothly. (Try to get personalized attention from Amazon about anything.) You may even be able to negotiate a discount from the bookstore, because bookstores get better pricing on business-to-business bulk sales. Despite its reputation for low prices, Amazon is slowly raising its prices on books, and it's hard to guarantee that they have enough stock in one place for any given bulk order. Bookstores can work directly with you and the publisher to ensure that everyone gets what they need. In exchange for a personal bulk-order concierge and a good price, the bookstore gets a nice sale to help them keep the lights on. Increasingly, bulk sales are an important part of bookstore profit and loss sheets, so sending your bulk orders through bookstores is a good way to protect them.

7. Preorder books from bookstores

Many authors and publishers have done a good job explaining the importance of preorders. For one thing, preorders can help a publisher gauge demand to ensure that there are enough copies of any given book in its first print run. Perhaps more importantly, a book's first-week sales total includes all the sales leading up to its release date in addition to the sales immediately after its release date. And a big fat first-week sales total gives the book a better chance of ending up on bestseller lists. Being on a bestseller list is a good indicator for staying on a bestseller list, and that first week is a book's best chance.

What folks have explained less effectively is that all preorders count as preorders. There's a lingering belief among authors and readers that the only preorders that "count" are on Amazon, and that's just not true. Bookstores report their sales to the same places Amazon does. Further, there are a few benefits to preordering from bookstores: often, an author's local bookstore will team up with the author to coordinate signed and dedicated copies of the book. Plus, bookstores are generally more conscientious about the condition of books, so if you're a first-edition collector you're better off ordering from a bookstore. When you preorder from bookstores, the bookstore gets the economic benefit of guaranteed sales, plus lots of helpful data about what books are going to hit it big.

8. Shop early for the holidays

In 2021 at the Raven, the fourth quarter accounted for 45% of the year's sales. Nearly half of our business happened in the last few months of the year, and we're not an anomaly in that regard. Driving this fall/winter sales bonanza, of course, is the Christmas holiday. But compounding the blitz is publishers' tendency to pack all the biggest releases into the end of the year. All of the post-presidency books by the Obamas have had November releases, for instance.

This means lots of good Christmas presents, sure, but it also means chaos for the bookstores trying to keep these books on the shelves. The complicated and fragile system used to make books is stretched thinner than ever. The global supply chain issues arising after the worst of the Covid-19 pandemic have been well documented, and bookstores feel that pain like everyone else. Contributing to this issue is a nationwide paper and printing shortage; just as paper is getting monstrously expensive, printing presses are shutting down. On top of all *that*, many of these high-profile fall books appear with very little notice and very large print runs, making it harder to print other books. This is all to say that if you're interested in helping your bookstore successfully capitalize on the vital fourth quarter, shopping early for Christmas is a great way to do it. For instance, starting your holiday shopping in October gives a bookstore more time to navigate supply chain chaos, ensuring that their shelves are fully stocked for the entirety of the fourth quarter.

9. Buy gift certificates from bookstores

Of course, if you can't manage to snag one of those hot fall titles, or if you're shopping for someone finicky who seemingly owns every possible book already, a gift certificate is a great way to go. From our end, gift certificates represent a literal investment in our future. The way gift certificate sales usually go, they are purchased in November and December and spent in trickles throughout the year. That leads to a big cash infusion for us during those crucial fourth-quarter months, allowing us to pay those big bills, give out employee bonuses, and hopefully eke out a little bit of profit. Gift certificates are one of the simplest ways to protect bookstores: paying for future books now.

10. Buy books from Bookshop.org

Bookshop.org is a startup alternative to Amazon, founded to sell books online in a way that helps bookstores. They're a certified B Corp, and their beneficiary is bookstores, which means they're contractually bound to give bookstores monetary support. Here's how Bookshop.org works: A bookstore can start an online storefront on Bookshop, adding branding and curated reading lists. The bookstore then earns 30% of each sale through their online storefront. Non-storefront sales also give a smaller percentage to bookstores. Additionally, regardless of whether a bookstore has a Bookshop storefront, they can get profit-pool payouts from Bookshop. On the fulfilment end, rather than going through a physical bookstore and its booksellers (see #1 on this list), Bookshop sales are processed by the warehouses of massive book wholesaler Ingram.

Reactions to Bookshop in the bookstore world are mixed. Some worry that Bookshop is taking away from direct bookstore sales, and others are concerned about the lower-than-normal margins on Bookshop sales. Still others worry about Ingram, a rapidly consolidating mega-corporation and the only large book wholesaler in the United States, gaining more power via direct-to-consumer sales. Others, however, celebrate Bookshop's ability to give people a start in the book industry without the massive investment needed for a brick-and-mortar storefront (see #37 on this list). A Bookshop storefront doesn't require a physical space; many bookstores that started during the Covid-19 pandemic began with a Bookshop storefront they used to raise money for further evolutions of their shops. This has enabled a huge number of new Black- and POC-owned bookstores to start up. The question of how much Bookshop. org protects bookstores is a complicated one, but I tend to take the view that a company that provides an easy alternative to Amazon and that has distributed $23 million to bookstores to date is a net good.

11. Follow bookstores on social media

When I started working on this zine in late 2022, Twitter was embroiled in a rushed takeover by Elon Musk, who seemed more interested in his own ego than in running a functional social media network. In another corner of the internet, Facebook and its subsidiary Instagram seem more interested in building a bad virtual reality world than any kind of good user experience. Also, literally as I was writing this section, Facebook announced 11,000 layoffs. TikTok just announced a plan to sell books directly to customers in the app, cutting out many of the bookstores who create content to make BookTok tick. I'm honestly not sure what the future holds for social media, and for bookstores on social media in particular. I say this with a bit of sadness as a bookstore owner (and, honestly, an author) who's achieved a bit of success thanks to social media. Though the future is uncertain, in the present, at least for now, social media remains one of the ways bookstores can connect with their communities online. On top of that, the flawed measure of follower count still holds some weight—for instance, if two stores are in contention to land a big author event, the publisher may use social media follower counts as a kind of tiebreaker. So before the whole thing teeters off into the digital void to make room for whatever's next, a good and free way to protect bookstores (and ensure they can communicate with their communities) is to follow a bunch of them on social media.

12. Tag, tweet, and talk to bookstores on social media

Here's one way the looming collapse of social media platforms has impacted bookstores: it's harder than ever for our stuff to get seen. Facebook is hell-bent on getting money from us in the form of sponsored posts. Instagram is so determined to be TikTok 2.0 that it's algorithmically burying any still photos.

Lord knows what's happening at Twitter (see #11 on this list). As far as I can tell, one way to help bookstores defeat the algorithm is for folks to talk to bookstores or tag them in their posts. Buying a book from a bookstore? Make an Instagram post about it and tag us (tag the author too, as long as you're saying nice things!). Feeling good in your bookstore merch? Tag us in the photo! This might help us avoid getting lost in the algorithm, sure. But even if it doesn't, it'll bring a smile to our faces.

13. Subscribe to bookstore newsletters

So if social media is growing less reliable or useful for bookstores trying to communicate with their communities, what's going to replace it? I can't speak for everyone, but I'll tell you the Raven is doubling down on our email newsletters. The newsletter format is much easier to cram with information. Even better, we can control who sees what without rolling the algorithmic dice (see #11). Lots of bookstores put really good stuff in their newsletters—staff reviews of forthcoming books, glimpses into the day-to-day operations of the business, event information, and more. From where I sit, the bookstore email newsletter is the best way to get information from a store, short of actually going in and asking someone a question. By subscribing to and reading a bookstore's newsletter, you are joining its community and therefore helping to protect it.

14. Be a reader

Here's maybe the easiest one on this list: read books. Make books a part of your life. You don't even need to buy them from bookstores. You can check them out of the library. You can raid the Little Free Library in your neighborhood. You can steal them from your family members while they're at work. You can even (gasp!) read the books you already own. The reasoning is simple: if America is a nation of readers, it will by extension be a nation of bookstores. It's not a huge leap for a lifelong reader to become a lifelong member of a bookstore's community.

I'm not going to soothsay about the doom-and-gloom End of Reading. I'm not going to weigh in on how much people watch TV or look at their phones. The death of the book has been predicted many times and will be predicted many times more. I'll just put it this way: reading begets reading. If you spend some time with a book today—even a few minutes!—you're already on the way to protecting bookstores.

15. Join a book club

A great way to help yourself become and stay a reader is to join a book club. Even if it's just an excuse to drink with friends. Even if you just meet online. Even if you just kvetch about the books. Even if Tyler's picks always kind of stink. Even if you talk about the book for 5 minutes and then spend the next 90 minutes gossiping about you-know-who. Even if it's only three members. A book club helps you turn your reading life into a community endeavor, and a community can sustain you as a reader. The more you're sustained as a reader, the more you'll read. The more you read, the more you'll protect bookstores (see #14).

16. Encourage your book club to team up with the bookstore

This list's suggestions about reading (#14) and book clubs (#15) are admittedly a bit indirect and non-economic. Fine. But here's a way book clubs *can* be an economic boon to bookstores: have your book club team up with your bookstore. We already know bulk sales can be a really good way to protect bookstores (see #6), and book clubs are a part of that equation. Once you've got some picks ironed out, let your local store know. They may order a bunch so you know they're there. They could set them aside under the name of your book club, or even give you a discount. Even at a discounted rate, those sales might still be worth it to them. A monthly guarantee of just 5 or 10 books sold to a local book club can make a huge difference, and it's one way your reading life can actively protect bookstores.

17. Get audiobooks from Libro.fm

Building a vibrant reading life helps protect bookstores (see #14). Fortunately, you don't even need physical books to do that! Audiobook readers can protect bookstores too. Sure, enemy-of-bookstores Amazon has a huge stranglehold on the audiobook market through their Audible platform: through Amazon's predatory consumer practices, as well as restrictive technology called digital rights management, Audible has claimed a gigantic share of the audiobook market, by some estimations upwards of 90%.[18] There's good news, though: a bookstore-friendly audiobook alternative exists. Libro.fm, a startup audiobook platform, has the same functionality and much of the same inventory as Audible. You subscribe, you get monthly credits, you use a mobile app. Only in Libro's case, a portion of your purchase goes to bookstores instead of to Jeff Bezos. You can even pick which bookstore gets the percentage of your sale. Helping bookstores stake a claim, no matter how small, in the Amazon-dominated audiobook market will help protect them.

---

18 Cory Doctorow, "We Need to Talk about Audible," *Publishers Weekly*, September 18, 2020, publishersweekly.com/pw/by-topic/industry-news/libraries/article/84384-we-need-to-talk-about-audible.html.

18. Move your online reviews away from Goodreads

Goodreads is owned by Amazon. Above all else, Amazon is a data company obsessed with gobbling up as much data about consumers as it possibly can. So when you rate a book on Goodreads, you're telling Amazon valuable info about your reading habits. Fortunately, as is the case with audiobooks (see #17) but not ebooks (see #33), there are bookstore-friendly alternatives for those seeking an online reader network. I personally like the StoryGraph. But which platform you migrate to isn't as important as divesting from Amazon. Goodreads is a deeply flawed platform with little to no safeguards against spamming negative reviews, which can and does lead to coordinated attacks against authors. Despite this, Amazon has begun including Goodreads reviews on Amazon book product pages. The idea is simple: readers handing over free data to Amazon makes it easier for Amazon to sell books to readers. The more books Amazon sells, the more of a grip it has on the US book market. To protect bookstores, stop giving Amazon free data about your reading. Anyway, it's much more rewarding and pleasant to share data about your reading life via conversation, perhaps with a book club (#15) or a bookseller (#22).

19. Read weird books

A bookstore won't carry the same books as a Walmart. You're much more likely to find translated books, small-press books, and otherwise surprising or weird books at a bookstore. As Jason Guriel writes in *On Browsing*, small bookstores "stacked the deck in favour of the quirky, the prickly, the heroically uncommercial. In favour of discovery."[19] Bookstores' proclivity for off-the-beaten-path books comes from the fact that bookstores are spaces that celebrate books, curated by people who love them. A good bookstore inventory specialist will lovingly work to fill their store with books that surprise and innovate. Sometimes, bookstores will collectively do this so well as to reverse-engineer an actual mainstream hit. Without the support of bookstores, Elena Ferrante's Neapolitan Novels wouldn't have found the massive mainstream audience they eventually did. Same goes for Robin Wall Kimmerer's now-classic *Braiding Sweetgrass*. Of note is the fact that both authors publish with independent small presses.

On a personal note, sales of *How to Resist Amazon and Why* far exceeded my wildest dreams thanks exclusively to bookstores' enthusiasm for the book. If readers show their hunger for weird, innovative, or surprising small-press books by buying them from bookstores, it's a clear message to the book industry at large that these books (and the stores that sell them) are important. Discovering and advocating for under-the-radar books is one of the most important functions

---

19 Jason Guriel, *On Browsing* (Windsor: Biblioasis, 2022), 52.

of bookstores, and keeping demand high is a good way to protect bookstores and the work we do.

20. Bring your kids

Given that bookstores rely on communities of readers (see #14 on this list), an important way to protect bookstores is to nurture young readers so they will remain readers as adults. If you'll allow me to get personal once again, I have a son who's four as of this writing. One of the greatest joys of parenting so far has been to share a love of books with him. I was afraid he'd somehow not care about books, but it turns out all it took to make him fall in love with reading was . . . reading. We made books part of his routine, making sure to read at least a few with him every day. We go to the library and let him pick out whatever he wants. We spend time in bookstores, of course. This is a wonderful rhyme of history, as the origin of my own story involves my aunt Pat taking me to the Borders in Solon, Ohio. Every time Aunt Pat was in town, we went to Borders, and she made sure we didn't leave empty-handed. It doesn't even matter what the books were. The joy of a beloved family member spending quality time with me surrounded by books was enough to hook me as a reader forever. Bring your kids to the bookstore; it's the best way to ensure they'll keep coming back.

21. Bring your dates

Bearing in mind that I perhaps care about bookstores more than almost everyone else on earth, I still maintain that there's no better place to bring a date. There's lots to talk about, for one thing. If the conversation ever lags, a familiar title or favorite book can quickly get things going again. Plus, you can't beat the vibes in a bookstore. We work really hard on that. Low music. Soft lighting. Lots of corners. It's romantic, and we know that (please don't do anything too untoward in those corners). Plus, in terms of getting to know someone, how better than by learning about their favorite books? It could go both ways: The dude you're on a first date with could reveal his fondness for Jordan Peterson, a useful red flag. Alternately, you could discover a shared love for the early novels of Zadie Smith, instantly growing closer, which in an indirect but not insignificant way leads you to get married and start a family you can bring to the same bookstore (see #20). And how does all this protect bookstores? Why, folks in the store on Friday nights. A busy bookstore is a bookstore that will stick around.

22. Ask for help

For all the Silicon Valley whizbangery that goes into a Kindle, or Amazon's search algorithm, or any number of other attempts to techify bookselling, tech bros have yet to invent anything that's better at selling books than an actual human. A good book recommendation is a bit of magic, because there's a lot that goes into it. A reader won't want something exactly like the last book they read, because that'll be boring. You can only recommend the same author until the reader reads all that author's books. People love to be surprised, but there are lots of bad ways to be surprised—a lover of sweet rom-coms may be surprised by the thoughtful gore in a novel by Stephen Graham Jones, but not necessarily in a good way. But then again, the right romance reader might actually pounce on a good horror book. It's impossible for a computer to know. It's even difficult for a human to do, but certainly not impossible, especially if that human is a clever bookseller. Any given bookstore is likely filled with several of these clever booksellers, and watching them do their work is a thrill that will enrich your reading life. At the Raven, a lot of the booksellers have "fans" that follow all of their recommendations. Literally as I write this, a Raven colleague just texted me: a customer came in to say the last seven books they read were all staff picks from the same bookseller.

Recommendation seeking protects bookstores because it's job security: the more people take advantage of recommending, our most important skill and the one that cannot be digitally replaced, the more demand there is for our services. That turns into sales, of course (see #1 on this list), but it also turns into more perceived value for what we do. Publishers, authors, and other book industry folks will notice and appreciate the skill and value of our work, which will go a long way towards ensuring our future.

II. HOW POLICYMAKERS AND THOSE IN POWER CAN HELP

*T*he idea that "voting with your dollar" can solve systemic and societal issues is a bit of a neoliberal fiction. Granted, spending money at a bookstore will help make sure that bookstore will stick around. That's important. But spending money at a bookstore won't solve, for instance, corporate greed or white supremacy. An individual choice (say, buying fancy light bulbs) cannot solve a systemic problem (the climate crisis) when the systemic problem is caused by corporate interests and the failure of policy to deal with them. The corporations and politicians might *want* you to think that light bulbs will solve the climate crisis, but it's a smokescreen designed to pull the focus away from their gobbling up of money and failure to implement policy. Same goes for the challenges and problems facing bookstores: while your dollar is a show of support to bookstores, and bookstores need that, the long-term solution to problems caused by corporate greed and bad antitrust policy is policy, not individual spending choices.

With that in mind, the second section of this zine is composed of policy solutions that would make significant progress towards protecting bookstores, as well as a few other things non-political power-holders can do, too. If you're a politician reading this, working to implement these policies is the best way for you to protect bookstores. If you're not a politician, you can certainly be in touch with your elected officials at all levels of government to tell them that bookstores (and small businesses and the climate and human rights) are important to you.

23. Break up Amazon

Amazon remains the biggest roadblock to the success of all retail small businesses, including bookstores. This is true because of their massive market share in everything from shoes to books to video camera doorbells, and their anticompetitive tactics in those markets. Here are two strategies Amazon uses to build and keep that massive market share: First, predatory pricing. Amazon heavily discounts retail goods, forcing their competitors out of business. Then, they slowly raise prices. This is common monopoly behavior, and it's not particularly legal, but it's very rarely prosecuted (see #24). Another Amazon monopoly-building behavior might be easier to handle legally: being a platform and competitor at the same time. Amazon Marketplace, which represents billions of dollars in revenue and a majority of Amazon's retail sales, works like this: Amazon lets small businesses sell things on their Amazon Marketplace website in exchange for some fees, which often exceed an exorbitant 30% of each purchase.[20] The problem is, Amazon also sells their own Amazon-branded products on Amazon Marketplace, giving them key advantages. Free advertising, for one. For another, a trove of product data that they use (read: steal) to make their own competing products. This is fundamentally unfair, and it has allowed Amazon to basically take over the entire ecommerce market. Making it illegal to both host and sell on a platform would be a major step towards protecting bookstores and other small businesses. A bill to do just that, the American Innovation and Choice Online Act, started to move through Congress in 2021, but failed to receive a full vote in either the House or the Senate. As of 2023, with a Republican-controlled House, its prospects are uncertain.

24. Stronger antitrust enforcement

Aren't monopolies illegal? Isn't the government supposed to intervene to prevent anticompetitive behavior in free markets? Yes. But here's the problem: for the last four decades, the enforcement of antitrust law has been totally kneecapped in favor of letting big companies get as big as they want. In the 1970s and 1980s, far-right economist and judge Robert Bork introduced a radical new interpretation of antitrust law: rather than encouraging competition, antitrust law should focus on what he called "consumer welfare." In plain language, that means regulators shouldn't worry about how big companies are, as long as the companies keep prices low. This thinking was embraced by the influential Chicago School of Economics and, ultimately, Ronald Reagan. And so we find ourselves at the tail end of four decades of flaccid antitrust enforcement. Since the 1980s, if a company can prove they're lowering prices, they're free to get as big as they want and there's nothing regulators can do. Hence, it's hard to stop Amazon from being so big and anticompetitive because Amazon generally has low prices on retail goods (though they often raise them after putting their competitors out of business; see #23). A good policy switch to protect bookstores is to return to a more pro-competitive theory of antitrust law, where a company's holistic competitive effects are the basis for antitrust enforcement.

Fortunately, there's some exciting movement in this regard. The Biden administration has been sympathetic to those calling for antitrust reform, as reflected most clearly in a few appointments of key neo-antitrust folks like FTC chair Lina Khan and DOJ Antitrust Division head Jonathan Kanter. This reinvigorated antitrust movement faced its first major test in trying to block the merger of mega-publishers Penguin Random House and Simon & Schuster. Notably, the DOJ's case focused on the deal's hindering competition, not its pricing effects. The DOJ won handily, with Judge Florence Pan eviscerating

---

20 Stacy Mitchell, *Amazon's Toll Road* (Institute for Local Self-Reliance, 2021), 4.

the publishers' case in a blistering opinion that claimed that "the effect of [the proposed merger] may be substantially to lessen competition."[21] This is a big deal, and it may represent a turning point in antitrust enforcement. In a statement, Institute for Local Self-Reliance co-director Stacy Mitchell said the ruling represented "the beginning of the end of the consumer welfare standard, which has warped and enfeebled antitrust enforcement for the last 40 years."[22] After the decision came down, *Vulture* blogger Victoria Bekiempis called out what many in the book industry were also thinking: that Amazon surely must be next. She writes, "The elephant in the room throughout all of this continues to be Amazon, as the Big Five still seemingly feel like David to Amazon's Goliath. With this merger now blocked, Amazon continues to write everyone's rules."[23] A reinvigorated antitrust movement, focused on competition rather than pricing, would go a long way towards protecting bookstores.

25. Universal healthcare

Nothing on this list is a silver bullet. I can't point to one of these 50 items and say, "That one. That's the one that'll save bookstores." But if you held a gun to my head and told me to pick the one that would come closest, it could be this: national universal healthcare. Health insurance and the cost of healthcare create a massive challenge for both bookstore owners and the people who work for them. It's a humongous expense—far too high. By some measures the US spends more money per capita on healthcare than anywhere else in the world.[24] How much is this a pain in the ass? Let me count the ways. First, bookstores operate on super thin margins, and offering health coverage for employees eats into that. Second, if health insurance is tied to employment, the natural incentive is to find jobs that offer it, and independent literary retail has a harder time affording it than other sectors. We're losing talented, passionate people because we can't

21 Victoria Bisset, "Judge Blocks Simon & Schuster and Penguin Random House Merger," *Washington Post*, November 1, 2022, washingtonpost.com/business/2022/11/01/penguin-random-house-simon-schuster-merger-blocked/.

22 Stacy Mitchell and Reggie Rucker, "'The Beginning of the End of the Consumer Welfare Standard,' Stacy Mitchell Says of Blocked Merger of Penguin Random House and Simon & Schuster," Institute for Local Self-Reliance, November 1, 2022, ilsr.org/statement-penguin-random-house-simon-schuster-merger-blocked/.

23 Victoria Bekiempis, "Judge Shuts Book on Penguin Random House–Simon & Schuster Merger," *Vulture*, November 1, 2022, vulture.com/2022/11/judge-blocks-prh-simon-schuster-merger.html.

24 Emma Wager, Jared Ortaliza, and Cynthia Cox, "How Does Health Spending in the U.S. Compare to Other Countries?" Health System Tracker, January 1, 2022, healthsystemtracker.org/chart-collection/health-spending-u-s-compare-countries-2/#GDP%20per%20capita%20and%20health%20consumption%20spending%20per%20capita,%202020%20(U.S.%20dollars,%20PPP%20adjusted).

pay for health insurance. And if a bookstore owner does offer health insurance, it might mean lower wages.

Let's get personal: I believe in offering the best possible jobs to the Raven's booksellers, even in the face of my industry's tight margins and lack of support for stores like mine. So, in 2019 I set out to offer health insurance. The messy business of trying to make that happen took me more than a year to figure out. A traditional group plan was far too expensive—simply out of reach if I wanted to offer plans that didn't have staggeringly high deductibles. On top of that, for some of my employees, taking health coverage from the Raven would've *cost them money*. You see, the group plan would've been more expensive than plans they could get on the Affordable Care Act marketplace, but the mere act of my offering a group plan would've made them ineligible for those ACA plans! Basically, they would've needed to take a financial hit in order to get worse insurance. What we ended up settling on was something called an ICHRA, a plan that reimburses employees for their existing coverage. It's not nothing, but it's not ideal. I still have to ask employees to fight through the thicket of finding their own plans. Some of the plans offered by the ACA have high enough deductibles to be functionally useless.

The American healthcare system is beyond broken in so many ways; one of them is that it makes it very hard for bookstores to give their employees the health coverage they deserve. If everyone simply got universal single-payer health coverage from the government, it would alleviate so much stress and expense for small businesses. Talk about antitrust all you want (and if you've read this far, you know I certainly will), but the quickest, most pragmatic policy suggestion that would bring instant relief to every single bookstore, no exceptions? Universal healthcare. No question.

26. Worker-friendly legislation

It is a core belief of this project that the future of bookselling is booksellers. Here's what I mean: if people can't make decent careers as booksellers, then bookstores will suffer. A bookstore with happy, well-compensated employees is a bookstore built for the future. A bookstore that can't retain talented people is doomed to an endless cycle of hiring, training, and dealing with employees who aren't particularly dedicated to the store or bookstores in general. An entire industry built on low wages, long hours, and high turnover is a house of cards waiting to collapse in the slightest breeze. I strongly believe that what's good for workers is good for bookstores, and my own experience at the Raven has borne this out.

Not everyone agrees with me. Some bookstores, facing unionization efforts, have declined to voluntarily recognize the unions or have even engaged in unionbusting tactics. Some bookstore owners might argue that unionizing is too expensive, because higher wages would cut into the oft-discussed thin margins. They say that involving a union prevents direct communication between management and rank-and-file employees. These folks would probably argue that protecting the right to unionize is in fact the opposite of protecting bookstores.

I disagree. If there's no future for workers in bookstores to engage in well-compensated, rewarding, safe work, then there's no future for bookstores. There are lots of ways for workers to advocate for such a future. Unions can be one of them. It follows that one way to protect bookstores is by legally shoring up the power of unions—for example, by repealing so-called "right-to-work" laws. There's hope for worker-friendly legislation: in the 2022 midterm elections, Illinois voters easily added a workers' rights amendment to the state constitution.

Forming a union is one thing; negotiating a contract is another. The past few years have featured some amazing union-formation successes. For example, hundreds of unions have formed at Starbucks stores nationwide. And, stunningly, the JFK8 Amazon Fulfillment Center on Staten Island successfully unionized with the startup Amazon Labor Union. Yet holding a successful vote is just the first step. Companies like Amazon and Starbucks (and perhaps some bookstores) might delay, resist, and otherwise filibuster the contract process through legal maneuvering, endless appeals to the National Labor Relations Board, and other unionbusting tactics. This isn't hypothetical: as I write this, unionized employees at Big Five publisher HarperCollins are currently in the middle of an indefinite strike after working without a contract since April 2022. The government can and should be there to help unions deal with this corporate behavior. A fair and equitable union contract means security for a bookstore, because properly compensated employees who feel safe and seen at work are the best investment a bookstore can make in its future. One way the government can help ensure a good future for bookstores, then, is to interpret and enforce labor law in a way that protects even the smallest of unions from even the most ruthless of unionbusting campaigns.

27. Federal book fund

For this idea, I turn to our neighbors to the north. Fun fact: the Canadian Government offers millions of dollars in grant funding to make sure Canada has a healthy book industry. A branch of the Department of Canadian Heritage, the Canada Book Fund (CBF) for the past 40 years . . . has been the Government of Canada's main support mechanism for the Canadian-owned book publishing industry. The objective of the CBF is to ensure access to a diverse range of Canadian-authored books, nationally and internationally, by fostering a strong industry that publishes and markets Canadian-authored books.[25] The CBF has supported all kinds of Canadian literary initiatives in its decades of work. Typically, the support has gone towards Canadian publishers and literary organizations. With the advent of the Covid-19 pandemic, the CBF added a third focus: booksellers. The first CBF bookseller-supporting initiative awarded $12 million CAD to 180 booksellers (operating 467 locations) to better facilitate the selling of books online. All told, from 2012 to 2018, the CBF awarded $220.6 million CAD in grants and support, according to the Department of Canadian Heritage. This is a perfectly clear example of how the government can help protect bookstores by giving them money to help them solve their problems. But I can already hear the opposition to this idea: government spending is out of control. In response, a quick calculation. The CBF's $220 million over six years equals about $37 million CAD a year. $37 million CAD is the cost of 7.5% of one F22 fighter jet. Six years of funding for the Canadian Book Fund is about 1/4 of what the NYPD spends on overtime in a single year.[26] Mind you, the US is a far larger country with a far higher GDP, so $37 million CAD a year wouldn't go quite as far here. Still, even that much would allow a lot of book dreams to come true while representing a statistically insignificant cost for the government.

I should note that the US's National Endowment for the Arts does have literary initiatives. However, their funding goes to individual authors, as well as literary nonprofits. These are both worthy causes, for sure, but this structure makes it impossible for bookstores to directly benefit from NEA funding unless they're set up as a nonprofit. The clearest example I can give to illustrate the difference between how the Canadian government funds books and how the American government does it is this: When I just now looked at the copyright page of the nearest Canadian small-press book (Jason Guriel's *On Browsing* from Biblioasis), I saw an acknowledgement of the Canada Council for the Arts as well as a few other government agencies. On the copyright page of the nearest American small-press book (Saeed Jones's *Alive at the End of the World* from Coffee House Press), I saw the NEA logo, yes, but also logos for Target and

25 Canadian Heritage, *Evaluation of the Canada Book Fund, 2012–13 to 2017–18* (Canadian Heritage, 2019), vi.
26 Annie McDonough, "NYPD, Other Uniformed Agency Overtime Spending Is on the Rise," *City & State NY*, August 17, 2022, https://www.cityandstateny.com/policy/2022/08/nypd-other-uniformed-agency-overtime-spending-rise/375996/.

Amazon. Funding for a healthy book industry is crucial—so crucial, in fact, that we cannot leave it up to corporations.

A national book fund like Canada's, with its explicitly stated holistic focus on the entire book ecosystem, would protect American bookstores. Here's an easy first initiative for the hypothetical American Bookstore Fund: grants for new bookstores, with a special focus on booksellers from marginalized backgrounds. This would instantly erase the bookstore industry's high-cost barrier to entry, which is the single biggest obstacle for the next generation of booksellers (see #37 on this list).

28. Minimum wage increases

You may think I'm arguing two different things when I say both "bookstores don't make enough money" and "minimum wage should go up." But, as I've said elsewhere (see #26, for instance), a bookstore's best investment is the people that work there. Some bookstores increase wages voluntarily; the Raven's starting wage is well more than double the federal minimum wage, for instance, and we do everything we can to ensure employees are at or above the living wage for our county. But being able to guarantee that any job, bookstore or otherwise, pays a living wage is one way for government to protect small businesses. I understand the opposing argument, that making cash-strapped businesses spend even more on payroll may lead to cuts or even businesses shutting down. But researchers at UC Berkeley have found that "a higher minimum wage can produce benefits not just for workers, but for their employers, their communities and the entire economy."[27] After all, raising compensation for all workers means the potential to create more customers and thus more revenue. If people are making more money, they have more money to spend at places like bookstores. Raising the minimum wage would be a step towards embracing the radical notion that people who work at bookstores should be able to afford shopping at them.

29. Minimum shipping-cost legislation

In many ways, France is a model for policy strategies to protect bookstores. As of Fall 2022, it's now illegal to charge less than €3 to ship a book in France.[28] The government had already outlawed free shipping, but in response, Amazon and other mega-retailers began charging €0.01 for shipping. The French government responded to this by creating a minimum book-delivery fee. This is an example

---

27 Edward Lempinen, "A $15 Minimum Wage Would Cost Jobs, Right? Probably Not, Economists Say," *Berkeley News*, March 18, 2021, https://news.berkeley.edu/2021/03/18/a-15-minimum-wage-would-cost-jobs-right-probably-not-economists-say/.
28 Angelique Chrisafis, "France Sets Minimum Book Delivery Fee in Anti-Amazon Struggle," *The Guardian*, September 23, 2022, https://www.theguardian.com/world/2022/sep/23/france-minimum-book-delivery-fee-amazon.

of good policy that's explicitly designed to protect bookstores. One of Amazon's most pernicious impacts on the retail market is the proliferation of what they call free next-day shipping. Amazon's shipping structure creates the perception that things should be shipped very fast and for free. This is impossible for anybody else to keep up with. For one thing, the only reason Amazon can swing it is because they create incredibly dangerous warehouse conditions in order to ship so fast; for another, Amazon's huge portfolio of revenue streams (like the exorbitant fees on marketplace sellers—see #23) allows them to lose money on shipping retail goods. But in reality, shipping is not free, and it's not really fast, either. It's not a controversial statement to say it takes time and money to send objects to other places. A minimum shipping charge on online purchases would reintroduce the idea that shipping does in fact cost money, thus allowing bookstores to better compete.

30. Maximum book-discount legislation

France has bookstore protecting figured out in one other crucial way besides outlawing free shipping (see #29). Since 1981, it's been illegal to discount a book more than 5% in France. Again, this law was passed with the explicit purpose of protecting bookstores, and there's evidence that it worked. Despite having only 20% of the US's population, France has more bookstores.[29] It's hard to imagine this book-discount law didn't have something to do with that. After all, how can a monopolizing mega-corporation (or even a regular bookstore chain) engage in predatory pricing if they can't discount a book more than 5%, just like everyone else? If enacted here, these two French policies—minimum shipping fee and maximum discount—would instantly ease Amazon's grip on the book market and dramatically level the playing field for bookstores. (Before I get yelled at for saying books should be more expensive, remember that I'm also arguing that everyone should make more money [see #28] and that public libraries are cool [see #46]).

31. Better publisher discounts

This one is for the publishers. When a bookstore orders a book from a publisher, the average wholesale discount is 40–46%. That's an issue for a few reasons. First off, it represents a smaller markup than many other retail goods. This is what booksellers mean when they say our industry has "razor-thin margins"; we make less, percentage-wise, than many of our other retail peers. Second, it's fairly common for Amazon to list popular books at bookstores' wholesale

29 Angelique Chrisafis, "Bookshops Thrive as France Moves to Protect Sellers from Amazon," *The Guardian*, November 1, 2021, https://www.theguardian.com/world/2021/nov/01/bookshops-thrive-as-france-moves-to-protect-sellers-from-amazon.

prices. If a bookstore wants to sell a copy of N.K. Jemisin's new book *The World We Make*, the store writes a check to Hachette for $16.20 and sells it for the sticker price (which is printed right there on the book) of $30. Right now, Amazon is selling the book to consumers for $15.99. I'd never do it, of course, but it'd actually be cheaper for me to order this book from Amazon than from the publisher wholesale. There are lots of policy suggestions that would solve this problem at the Amazon level (see #24 and #30, for instance). To solve it at the bookstore level, publishers could simply give better prices to bookstores. We hear all the time from publishers, sales reps, and publicists that bookstores are vital to publishers; though we're a small market, they say, we're vital for things like discoverability and connecting with readers. One way publishers could prove their love of bookstores is to give bookstores a 10% better wholesale price. It would unlock lots of possibilities for us, chief among them being to offer higher wages and better benefits.

32. Better landlords

I've talked to a bookseller who showed up to their rented storefront one day to find it padlocked, with all their inventory still inside. The owner had foreclosed on the property without informing its tenant, the bookstore, of any financial straits. I've talked to a bookstore owner who, just that day, had received a letter that doubled their rent, forcing them to find a new location two months before Christmas. Even aside from these drastic examples, just the fact of sky-high commercial rents is putting a strain on many, if not most, bookstores. Again, this list has no silver bullets on it, but I guarantee that if you could press a button that instantly halved the rent for every bookstore in the country, it would be a game changer for the future of bookstores in America.

I'll try to be charitable about this and imagine a reason for the rent crisis other than simple greed. I suppose there could be lots of explanations. If you ask a landlord, they'll probably blame city policy or property tax payments or building maintenance costs. Granted, I suppose it is possible that some terrible landlords are not being terrible on purpose—that property taxes and other city policies are indeed forcing them to charge exorbitant rates to small-business tenants. If that's the case, though, small businesses should not bear the costs. Rather, those city policies need to change. This isn't a debate, it's a crisis. Landlord issues range from "pain in the ass" (maintenance issues, building condition, rents that are too high) to existential (being forced to move because of rent or other factors). Across the country, exorbitant commercial rents are threatening the fabric of urban life. The introduction to this zine makes the case that small businesses, especially bookstores, provide countless economic and cultural benefits to their communities. A landlord who is also a good local citizen, then, will find it in their interest to make it possible for a bookstore to operate in their space. For the first 30 years of the Raven's history, we had a landlord who charged well below market rate on rent simply because he thought it was good for a bookstore to be in that building. Why aren't there more landlords like this, who view the existence of a bookstore as the community investment it actually is? Under no circumstances should it make sense for a landlord to keep a storefront empty. Under no circumstances should a bookstore have to shut down because it can't pay its impossibly high rent. Whatever needs to change to end that, it needs to change now.

33. A bookstore-friendly ebook solution

While there's a bookstore-friendly alternative to Amazon's chokehold on the audiobook market (see #17), its grip on the ebook market is even stronger, and, unfortunately, there isn't a one-size-fits-all alternative. According to Rebecca Giblin and Cory Doctorow's book *Chokepoint Capitalism*, Amazon has built an "enduring chokepoint" of the ebook market, having captured "fully 90 percent" of ebook sales a mere two years after the introduction of the Kindle and refusing to let up since.[30] For all intents and purposes, Amazon remains the only way to read ebooks. This was a calculated objective that Amazon spent years working towards: early on, Jeff Bezos told an executive working on the Kindle project to "proceed as if your goal is to put everyone selling physical books out of a job."[31] Basically, Amazon ebooks have super restrictive digital rights management (DRM) that only lets them be viewed on devices or apps that Amazon manufactures. Further, because of DRM, you never actually buy an ebook from Amazon. Rather, you essentially lease the right to access it. Amazon sells this access, as well as the devices needed to use it, at predatorily low prices. To achieve these low prices, Amazon bullies publishers into contracts that allow this monopolizing long game to happen.

At one point, much too late, four major US publishers got together to fight back against Amazon's unfair ebook practices. In response, US antitrust enforcers punished *the publishers* for anticompetitive behavior. This as Amazon established near-total control over the ebook sector. As Giblin and Doctorow put it, "The publishers were affronted. How could *they* be liable for anticompetitive conduct when they only did what they did to counteract Amazon's own bullying? But that's how it currently works."[32] (For more information about the flawed way

30 Rebecca Giblin and Cory Doctorow, *Chokepoint Capitalism* (New York: Beacon Press, 2022), 27.
31 Giblin and Doctorow, *Chokepoint Capitalism*, 24.
32 Giblin and Doctorow, *Chokepoint Capitalism*, 31.

antitrust law "currently works," see #24 on this list). Now that Amazon has captured nearly all of the ebook market, it's really hard to convince people to switch. They've spent years building libraries that aren't compatible with any other platforms. Because Amazon isn't removing their DRM anytime soon, users would have to start over fresh if they switched. Giblin and Doctorow call this a "cost moat" and it's a key advantage tech monopolies use to stay in power: switching to a non-monopolizing, bookstore-friendly alternative would just be too expensive.

Bottom line: Consider this a call to venture capitalists, software writers, tech engineers, and mechanical minds better than mine. To really protect bookstores, build a bookstore-friendly ebook platform that somehow allows Amazon users to switch without losing entire libraries.

III. ACTICE COMMUNITY MEMBERSHIP

*T*he third section of this zine centers on how you can engage with your community and take collective action to protect bookstores. While the individual purchasing choices and online habits laid out in section I are certainly impactful, and the policy suggestions in section II are a major piece of the puzzle, you can also make a real difference by taking action as a conscious participant in a wider community—whether that's your neighborhood, your city, or a labor organization. This section offers suggestions for how to do just that.

34. Spend time wandering the neighborhood

A quick story: After a series of increasingly aggressive sales calls from online review aggregator Yelp, I broke down and finally listened to their pitch. They wanted me to pay $25,000 a year for advertising to ensure the Raven appeared first in Yelp search results. Thus, we'd appear above what they considered our competition, the Dusty Bookshelf down the street. We said no. First of all, our entire yearly marketing budget, which we calculate based on industry averages, is less than half of $25,000. Second, of course, we don't view the Dusty Bookshelf as our competition. This is a key difference between the Silicon Valley view of things (Yelp) and the small-business view of things (the Raven): we believe a rising tide raises all ships. If our neighbor businesses are thriving, so are we. We are rooting for all the other shops and restaurants on our street because our business model is built on a steady stream of sidewalk traffic past (and hopefully through) our door. A great way to build that traffic is to have lots of small businesses in a small area of town. So here's another cheap and easy way to protect bookstores: go downtown and wander.

35. Be active in local politics

One way to build a small district filled with thriving small businesses (see #34 on this list) is to wander around and patronize the small businesses in your town. But, again, I never want to pin too much responsibility on individuals and their purchasing power. The struggles that small businesses face in America in 2023 are indeed systemic issues (see #23–33 on this list). Wandering around and spending money does help, but even more important are smart development, small-business-friendly strategic planning, and other municipal political strategies. The decisions of what gets built, how, and where can have massive repercussions for the bookstores and small businesses in your community. Similarly, tax legislation can have an outsized impact on those businesses' slim margins (see #4 and #31 on this list).

Here's a scenario that's repeated itself time and again in American cities for more than a decade: Amazon decides to build a new fulfillment center and rolls into town promising thousands of new jobs. They politely ask for tax breaks wherever they can find them, and local governments are happy to oblige. This is not a way to protect bookstores and other small businesses. The American Booksellers Association (ABA) has reported that Amazon fulfillment centers have drastically displaced jobs and economic activity from downtown districts to industrial parks on the perimeters of towns and cities. The ABA provides a memorable illustration of this impact: Take the physical area and economic activity of the Mall of America. Multiply it by 300. That's how much economic activity Amazon's warehouses have displaced away from downtowns and into anonymous industrial parks on the outskirts.[33] It's a bizarre twist on the story of shopping malls, which similarly pulled economic activity away from downtown. But this time around, the malls, having failed, are being leveled to build Amazon warehouses. If you find all this alarming, tell your local city councilperson. Perhaps while you're wandering around downtown, you can stop by city hall for a public comment explaining how important small businesses are. Write a letter, pen an op-ed, vote in local elections, do what you can to make it known to your local politicians that thriving small businesses (including bookstores) are important to you.

36. Use public transit

Here's one thing you can talk to your local government (see #35) about: public transit. A pedestrian-friendly downtown is crucial for small businesses, which can sink or swim depending on a neighborhood's sidewalk traffic (see #34). The shift to car-based urban design in the 20th century coincides exactly with the exodus of commercial activity away from downtown and towards interstates and urban peripheries. To regain density and energy in urban downtowns, pedestrian-friendly urban planning is a must. Investing in public transportation is a major and direct step in ensuring that downtown commercial districts can thrive. Therefore, using and advocating for public transit is a way to protect bookstores.

37. Make it easier for people to start small businesses

In 1986 and 1987, when college friends Pat Kehde and Mary Lou Wright decided they wanted to open a bookstore in Lawrence, Kansas, they talked to several banks. None of the banks offered them business loans. A few dismissed their idea as a hobby, not a business. Despite the lack of financing, their business persists to this day as the Raven Book Store, my bookstore home. You know what else

33 ABA and Civic Economics, *Unfulfilled*, 10.

persists? The difficulty in obtaining startup funds for small businesses, especially for women and people of color. Without access to generational wealth, the amount of money needed to successfully start and stock a bookstore is easily out of reach. Bank loans and support from the Small Business Administration require jumping through hoops and writing complex business plans. Gathering these materials can be a tremendous strain on someone who also has to work a full-time job to support themselves. Plus, applicants are easily denied even if all that stuff is ready to go. This functions as a barrier to entry, allowing only those who already have money to easily start up bookstores. There's no easy answer to this systemic issue, though a federal book fund as discussed in #27 would certainly help. Community-oriented solutions include micro-loans and crowdfunding (see #38). Really, any action that makes it easier for potential booksellers to acquire capital and start their businesses would be a critical step towards protecting bookstores.

38. Support bookstore crowdfunding efforts

From time to time, there's a really straightforward and direct way to protect bookstores: when bookstores ask for money online, give it to them (if you have the means). Given the difficulty of traditional financing, especially for women- and POC-owned bookstores (see #37), stores are turning to GoFundMe and other crowdfunding sites to raise capital to start, renovate, or simply continue their operations. Many bookstores have been saved by overwhelmingly positive responses to crowdfunding campaigns, especially at the uncertain and frightening beginning of the Covid-19 pandemic. Small donations coming together to raise a six-figure sum to save a bookstore is a perfect example of how individual choices together in community can create something bigger. Keep an eye out (bookstores usually announce fundraising efforts via newsletter [#13] and social media [#11]), and donate when you can.

39. Link up with organizations who are doing the work

Organizing and coalition building is an effective method for creating change, especially when the gears of policymaking move too slowly. In *Chokepoint Capitalism*, Rebecca Giblin and Cory Doctorow write, "The most important individual action you can take is to join a movement."[34] In the introduction to this zine, I mentioned how bookstores can introduce people to social movements because they're more durable than movement spaces like protests or occupations. Another entry point to social movements (like, for instance, a movement to protect bookstores and downtowns and small businesses and freedom of speech) is linking up with organizations that have a long history of activism. If you're concerned about the issues presented in this zine, and if

34 Giblin and Doctorow, *Chokepoint Capitalism*, 146.

you're committed to protecting bookstores, here are some organizations that are already doing good work. There's no single action that translates to support for every one of these organizations, but following them on social media and subscribing to their mailing lists is a great start. From there, let them tell you the ways they need support.

- The **American Booksellers Association** has, for more than a century, advocated to protect and enrich bookstores and the people who work in them. The ABA has a long history of pushing a pro-small-business policy agenda, from suing to fight unfair chain-bookstore pricing practices in the 1990s to being a leading voice in the new antitrust movement today.

- **Athena** is a coalition of labor organizations working to raise awareness about (and fight) Amazon's predatory practices.

- According to its website, the **Institute for Local Self-Reliance** is a think tank that "builds local power to fight corporate control," with focuses in antitrust, small business, local utility control, local broadband, and more. Their work has been instrumental in writing both this zine and *How to Resist Amazon and Why.*

- **PEN America** and the **National Coalition Against Censorship** are two groups working to combat the right-wing attack on freedom of speech.

- While the book industry historically has a low level of unionization, there are a few unions who represent different kinds of book workers. One Amazon warehouse is represented by the **Amazon Labor Union**. The **HarperCollins Union** is the only union at a Big Five publisher, and independent leftist press **Verso** is unionized. Other unionized publishers include the **New Press, Duke University Press, and Harvard University Press.** An increasing number of bookstores are unionized, including **Politics and Prose (Washington, D.C.), Greenlight Bookstore (Brooklyn), the Strand (New York City), Powell's Books (Portland, Oregon), Page 1 Books (Albuquerque), Skylight Books (Los Angeles), Moe's Books (Berkeley), Green Apple Books (San Francisco), Bookshop Santa Cruz (Santa Cruz), McNally Jackson (New York City), Book Culture (New York City), BookPeople (Austin), the Savoy Bookshop (Westerly, Rhode Island), and the Elliot Bay Book Company (Seattle).**

40. Donate to BINC

Here's one organization who is doing a world of vital work to help booksellers in the most direct way possible, an essential ally in a difficult and dangerous job (see #43). According to its website, the Book Industry Charitable Foundation (BINC) was founded with a mission of "assisting bookstore employees & comic retailers facing hardship & supporting career development." Any bookseller facing any kind of financial hardship can apply for BINC funds; the process is easy and fast. I've watched multiple Raven booksellers receive life-changing help from BINC. Yes, they accept donations. This is one of the most direct ways to protect bookstores on this entire list.

41. Vote for all that "best of the city" shit

I'm a bookseller, not a politician, so it feels weird for me to ask for votes. Still, every year I find myself encouraging folks to vote for the Raven in the local newspaper's "best of the city" contests. From a cynical perspective, these contests are a way to sell ads to the businesses featured in the thousands of categories, which isn't a surprise given the carnage unleashed upon the newspaper industry by big tech (see #49 for more). Still, ad grabs aside, the readership on this stuff is pretty high and some people do find us because we regularly win "best bookstore in Lawrence." Voting for your bookstore is one fast and free way to protect it.

42. Write good reviews online

Here's another thing I'm cynical about that nonetheless can help protect a bookstore. I don't put much faith in online reviews (see the Yelp anecdote in #34 on this list). The Raven is fortunate enough to have a pretty good set of reviews, and we're grateful for the positive ones. We're less grateful for the one-star reviews, many of which are unfair or nonsensical. (One called us a "woke joke"; another called me conceited. Still another claimed we were "mask nazis," which is a real fun thing for a Jewish bookseller to be called.) Still, there are those who do use a store's proximity to five stars as a metric when weighing whether or not to support it. Despite the flaws of the five-star industrial complex, a good online review is another fast and free way to protect a bookstore.

43. Be kind to retail and service workers

Since March 2020, countless public health enforcement decisions have fallen on hourly retail and service employees. For the last three years, every bookseller in the country has been in countless arguments about masks and vaccines. These conversations are not easy. I myself have been threatened (by a handwritten certified-mail letter, no less) because of my store's mask mandate.

Even without these post-2020 difficulties, bookstore work has always been hard. If you've been in retail or service, you know it. Long hours on your feet.

Difficult customers. Getting stuck in the weeds when the store is super busy. Physical pain. Mental exhaustion. I heard someone say that a US senator couldn't make it through a single peak shift at a Starbucks, and I believe it.

And of course, as discussed elsewhere, all of this happens while nobody doing it is making much money.

Yet we still do it. We have our reasons, from love to economic necessity to loyalty to stubbornness. But regardless of why a person happens to be working in a bookstore (or any retail/service environment), they are deserving of patience and respect. Here's what keeps booksellers going: when someone is kind or welcoming or interesting or fun, this job is worth it, despite its difficulties. One of the job's biggest rewards is the satisfaction of good interactions with kind and respectful customers. To protect bookstores, protect the dignity of those who work in them.

44. Support labor unions

You don't have to be a policymaker (#26) to support labor unions and their right to advocate for their members. As I write this, the only labor union at a Big Five publisher, the HarperCollins Union, is more than 50 days into an indefinite strike. The HC Union has widely circulated a list of steps that readers, authors, and booksellers can take to help support their efforts. Agents can hold off on sending pitches to HC editors. Booksellers can distribute bookmarks printed with union-supporting designs. Readers can post the union's graphics to their social media. People can donate directly to the union's strike fund. The HC Union even has a storefront on Bookshop.org, thereby giving folks a way to support bookstores and the union at the same time (see #10 on this list). All of these small steps are nonetheless steps towards ensuring a good future for workers in the book industry. (One important note is to always check if the union is calling for a boycott or not; the HC Union has expressly asked folks not to boycott, as a boycott could help management make the case that the union is bad for business. The best thing to do is subscribe to unions' social media or email newsletters and follow their lead in taking small steps to protecting a worker-friendly book industry.) Kim Kelly eloquently captures the crux of the issue: "If you love books, show love to the people who make them possible—and support their efforts to organize."[35] In a piece about bookstore unions for *Teen Vogue*, Kelly quotes Tove Holmberg, a veteran unionized bookseller at Powell's Books in Portland, Oregon:

> Bookstores get a lot of praise for being cultural hubs and community anchors; for promoting the open exchange of ideas; and for

---

35 Kelly, "Bookstore Workers."

championing progressive values; but so often, when bookstore workers voice concerns about their wages, benefits, or working conditions, that progressive facade falls away and an employer's true priorities are revealed. Book workers, like all workers, deserve to have a voice in their workplace, and the most powerful voice is the collective voice of a union.[36]

Bookstores and book workers face a complex web of challenges, but the fact remains that too many people working in books are not being properly or fairly compensated for their work. As the problem is complex, so are the solutions, but it's easy to see that collective action for book workers is one way to address the greed and consolidation driving the low wages in this industry.

45. Go to events at bookstores

Here's a great way to support bookstores that often doesn't include spending money at all: go to an event. Many bookstores host events. Some host hundreds per year. These are most often author events featuring a writer talking about their new book, but they can also be craft nights or book clubs or political organizing events. For one thing, attending an event makes you a part of that bookstore's community, and building a robust community is the bookstore's way of protecting its future. For another thing, the bookstore measures the success of events with the number of attendees, which often gets reported back to publishers. The publishers in turn look more kindly on bookstores that can provide big turnouts. Sure, we track sales, too, and the number one thing to do to help protect bookstores is to buy books there (see #1 on this list). But I can assure you that a bookstore will still be happy to see you at an event even if buying a book isn't in the cards for whatever reason.

46. Patronize your library

It's a little hard for me to believe, but it's true: I've heard that some bookstores don't have particularly good relationships with their libraries. The Raven and the Lawrence Public Library are best buds! We host events in their auditorium all the time. We sponsor their events and donate stuff to their fundraisers. They advertise on our walls. We sell books when they bring in big authors. In countless ways, LPL and the Raven work together to bolster literary life in our community, a clear example of rising-tide-raises-all-ships thinking (see #34). I don't think this arrangement is unique to Lawrence, Kansas, either. Libraries and bookstores have a lot of differences, but I maintain that they share at least one core goal: to build a community of engaged readers. We already know that a good way to protect bookstores is to place them within such a community. Libraries help

---

36 Kelly, "Bookstore Workers."

with that work. Alarmingly, though, libraries are increasingly under attack. For more about these attacks, and why libraries need to be protected right alongside bookstores, see #47 and #48 on this list.

47. Pay attention to attacks on libraries

Libraries are under attack, and it's easy to predict that bookstores are next. In late 2022 the St. Marys branch of the Pottawatomie Wabaunsee Regional Library in Kansas was up for a lease renewal on its building. Normally a routine local-government operation, this time around the library's lease renewal turned into a front in the culture wars. A parent in St. Marys was upset to find his child interested in Alex Gino's *Melissa*, a YA book with a transgender protagonist. The father insisted that, since it had a transgender character, nobody should be able to get this book from the St. Marys library. But before he could even submit a formal challenge to the library, the St. Marys City Council proposed a morality clause to be included in the library's lease. The clause stipulated that "the library not 'supply, distribute, loan, encourage, or coerce acceptance of or approval of explicit sexual or racially or socially divisive material, or events (such as "drag queen story hours") that support the LGBTQ+ or critical theory ideology or practice.'"[37] The library refused to sign the lease containing the clause, causing the city council to consider "creating their own city library, one without 'divisive material.'"[38] The situation came to a head in a series of city commission meetings in early winter 2022. Each time the commission met to discuss the issue, library supporters flooded the chambers in solidarity with the library and the tireless work of library director Judith Cremer.

Ultimately, the commission renewed the library's lease without restrictions, despite the months of threats. What made the difference? Public outcry and shows of support for the library. According to *Kansas Reflector* reporter Rachel Mipro, "Commissioners said the outpouring of public support for the library informed their decision to extend the lease by one year."[39] People showed up and made noise in support of the St. Marys library, and free speech in general, and it made a difference. This is how you save a library, and it's a playbook that can be used if (or when) bookstores face the same kinds of attacks: Show up. Make noise.

---

37 Rachel Mipro, "Future of Kansas Town's Library in Jeopardy over Refusal to Remove 'Divisive' Books," *Kansas Reflector*, November 14, 2022, https://kansasreflector.com/2022/11/14/future-of-kansas-towns-library-in-jeopardy-over-refusal-to-remove-divisive-books/.
38 Mipro, "Future of Kansas."
39 Rachel Mipro, "Kansas Town's Library Lease Renewed after Months of Debate about LGBTQ Content." *Kansas Reflector*, December 7, 2022, kansasreflector.com/2022/12/06/kansas-towns-library-lease-renewed-after-months-of-debate-about-lgbtq-content/.

This story has a happy ending for now, though I'm not resting easy about this issue. In St. Marys, even though the library can stay put for another year, they're certain to continue feeling pressure from the city commission. Radical right-wingers have been attacking libraries with alarming frequency nationwide; the St. Marys library is just one example that feels literally close to home for me. Of course, #46 and #20 on this list explain why libraries and young readers are both important for bookstores, but this issue goes beyond libraries. This is a crisis of community and free speech, a right-wing attack on difference and freedom itself. Yes, a staggering showing of public support was enough to save this library. I hope allies of libraries can gather like this each time a library comes under attack, and I hope they'll be ready when the attacks shift to bookstores.

48. Defend bookstores from right-wing attacks

In summer 2022, Virginia Republican politician Tommy Altman and his lawyer (and fellow Republican politician) Tim Anderson filed suit against Barnes & Noble. The alleged crime? Barnes & Noble simply carrying two books, *Gender Queer* and *A Court of Mist and Fury*. Anderson and Altman's suit claimed that the books were obscene and the stores needed parental consent before selling them to children. The suit was dismissed, but it represented a frightening escalation in a culture war that's raging across the country. In nearly every state, far-right reactionaries are working to prevent children from accessing certain books. These reactionaries have the endorsement of the national Republican Party in their efforts. It doesn't take Hercule Poirot to deduce that nearly all of the books in question feature queer characters or are written by queer, Black, Indigenous, or Latinx authors. The right-wing reactionaries trying to take over public libraries and school boards in the name of "protecting children" are not protecting children at all. Instead, these reactionaries are trying to force a heterosexual, white, regressive worldview on children by limiting what they can read.

Just to be clear: using the government to limit speech is an obvious violation of the First Amendment, and it's happening right now across the country. Librarians are being harassed, threatened, and forced out of their jobs. Entire libraries are at risk of shutting down in the face of these coordinated attacks (again, see #47). While these bans give some already-famous books a sales bump, they make it harder for countless other debut or midlist authors to sell books, creating yet another barrier for queer and BIPOC authors. Most alarmingly, LGBTQIA+ and BIPOC kids have a harder time seeing themselves in books, which may contribute to the serious mental health crisis affecting these groups. While the right-wing reactionaries' focus is currently on libraries, it could easily cross over into bookstores, which is why the Virginia lawsuit was so alarming. It's not enough to wear a little button that says, "I read banned books." To protect bookstores, we need to end the right-wing attack on books, and you can't do that with lapel pins alone.

One actionable way to protect bookstores is to show up and literally get in the way. In July 2022, a Drag Queen Story Hour hosted by Loyalty Bookstore in Silver Spring, Maryland, was disrupted by a group of far-right protestors. Founded in 2015 by author Michelle Tea, Drag Queen Story Hour (DQSH) is meant to engage kids with tolerance and literacy in a fun way that activates their imagination. The attack on Loyalty's event was not an anomaly: according to a report from GLAAD, there were at least 141 attacks on DQSHs in 2022 alone. The attacks are widespread, too, having occurred in all but two states.[40] On Twitter, Loyalty explained that their DQSH "was horribly interrupted by 'protestors' who invaded our space and screamed at children." The situation was serious enough that Logan Stone, the drag performer leading the event, had to be escorted away by booksellers as the children in attendance began to cry.[41] But Loyalty refused to buckle in the face of the Proud Boys' attack, and here's where your action step comes in: when Loyalty hosted their next DQSH a month later, counter-protestors lined the sidewalk at the event site. They held up rainbow flags, blocking any views of the event that far-right protestors might have.[42] Allies of the bookstore formed a literal human barrier protecting the children, the drag performers, and the booksellers from any further harassment. This is how you protect bookstores from hateful attacks.

49. Read and support local news

Local newspapers are in crisis. Here's a concise version of what happened: Craigslist killed newspaper classifieds, eliminating a crucial revenue source for local papers. Then the advertising arms of Amazon, Google, and Facebook killed newspaper ads altogether, eating up the ad money that used to pay for journalist salaries. Thus hobbled, local newspapers across the country found themselves in dire financial straits. This left them ripe for purchase by massive corporations, a few of which (like Gannett or Ogden) began gobbling up local papers. Even

40 Mary Emily O'Hara, "Updated GLAAD Report: Drag Events Faced at Least 141 Protests and Significant Threats in 2022," GLAAD.org, December 16, 2022, glaad.org/blog/updated-glaad-report-drag-events-faced-least-141-protests-and-significant-threats-2022.
41 Brandon Tensley, "Proud Boys Crashed Drag Queen Story Hour at a Local Library. It Was Part of a Wider Movement," CNN, July 21, 2022, cnn.com/2022/07/21/us/drag-lgbtq-rights-race-deconstructed-newsletter-reaj/index.html.
42 Dan Schere, "LGBTQ Activists Show Up to Support Drag Queen Story Hour at Brookside Gardens," *Bethesda Magazine*, August 13, 2022, bethesdamagazine.com/2022/08/13/lgbtq-activists-show-up-to-support-drag-queen-story-hour-at-brookside-gardens/.

worse, according to Cory Doctorow and Rebecca Giblin, "Many of these papers were purchased using a sketchy financial maneuver called a leveraged buyout; this saddles a paper with debt and commonly leads its new owners to adopt cost-saving measures like firing journalists and cutting arts coverage."[43]

Bookstores rely on local newspapers for many things. First, newspapers help drive event attendance and book sales when they write about certain books or authors. Second, the targeted, literary, hyper-local audience of a paper is one of the best advertising markets you could ask for. For another thing, a bookstore thrives best in a healthy community filled with engaged citizens, and it's hard to maintain that kind of community without a functioning local newspaper.

To add even more urgency to the question of bookstores and local newspapers, let's return to the story of the St. Marys library (#47 on this list). My main source for this story was coverage written by Rachel Mipro for the *Kansas Reflector*. The *Reflector* is a hyper-local, independent nonprofit news organization reporting on Kansas government issues, founded in the wake of the *Topeka Capital-Journal*'s 2017 sale to a newspaper-gobbling mega-corporation. The St. Marys article came to my attention because it was republished in another hyper-local nonprofit news publication, the *Lawrence Times*. The *LT* was founded by Mackenzie Clark, a former reporter for the *Lawrence Journal-World*, the legacy newspaper in the Raven's hometown of Lawrence, Kansas. Guess what? In 2016, the *Journal-World* was bought by Ogden, who then proceeded to empty its printing plant and impose dramatic cuts to staff.

In the interest of creating a local news outlet that was independent of monopolies, leveraged buyouts, and corporate control, Clark founded the *Lawrence Times*. It's interesting to note that the first, best, most thorough coverage of the St. Marys library attack came from the *Kansas Reflector* and the *Lawrence Times*, not the area's two monopoly-owned traditional newspapers. Without the dogged work of two small, independent news organizations, how much would this story be covered in Kansas at all? There are real-life consequences to this: the city commissioners themselves said public outcry is what kept the library alive; what kind of outcry can be mustered if the public doesn't know about the issue in the first place? So it's easy to imagine the story escaping notice, period, further silencing any queer or pro-free-speech voices in St. Marys.

Like so many other stories in this zine, the story of corporate media takeover and upstart local news outlets is playing out across the country. So what can this zine's reader do? It's one thing to subscribe to a newspaper limping along under the weight of a bad leveraged buyout and a distant corporate owner. But another crucial part of the work is supporting the people blazing a path towards

43 Giblin and Doctorow, *Chokepoint Capitalism*, 40.

what's next. Find the people writing the good stuff about your communities and read their work. Even better, pay for it (the Raven is a proud and longtime sponsor of the *Lawrence Times*, and I've contributed a few op-eds to the *Reflector*). It'll uplift your entire community, and the benefits will reach your bookstore and everyone else.

50. Ask big questions about the future of bookstores

I'd like to return to Kimberly Kinder's idea, cited in the intro, that bookseller activists "treat the [bookstore] as an enabling resource sustaining many functions through continual repurposing." I'm interested in both "many functions" and "continual repurposing." How can bookstores be reinvented to enable a thriving future for books, booksellers, and communities? Envisioning a bold future for bookstores is one way to protect them, because continual repurposing could be a path towards sustainability. I suspect an entire zine can be written on this alone, but here are some interesting questions to inspire you to imagine a more expansive bookstore future:

- Do we need landlords? The bookstore owner who one day found her inventory on the wrong side of a padlock just purchased that building, allowing her to wiggle out from under having a landlord at all. Also, Firestorm Books in Asheville, North Carolina, recently used crowdfunding to purchase a building. Immediately, they donated the land to a land trust, ensuring that predatory developers will never be able to build there.

- Do bookstores need to be for-profit businesses? Chicago's Seminary Co-op reinvented itself as a not-for-profit entity, the only nonprofit whose mission is selling books. Buffalo Street Books in Ithaca, New York, is a customer-owned co-op. Word Up Community Bookshop in Washington Heights, New York, is a 501(c)(3) nonprofit operated by a small staff alongside dozens of neighborhood volunteers. A feisty handful of radical co-op bookstores, like Baltimore's Red Emma's and NYC's Bluestockings, sell books outside of the traditional for-profit model. Many other bookstores, like St. Louis's Left Bank Books, have affiliated nonprofit entities that help further their missions.

- Do bookstores need to be in one permanent location? Cincinnati's Book Bus roves from festival to festival selling books. Milwaukee's La Revo Books draws from the Mexican mercado tradition to meet their customers at the community events where they're already gathering.

- Do bookstores even need to sell books? Rapper Noname expanded her popular online social justice book club into the Radical Hood Library, a worker-owned LA storefront lending library. Radical lending libraries are interesting to me; the SWAP Book Co-op in Oberlin, for instance, allows students to get textbooks for free in exchange for book donations or shifts manning the "store." Then there's Gainesville's Civic Media Center, a radical lending library focusing on zines. Can a radical lending library do the same community work as a bookstore without forcing radical activists to operate within capitalism? And can a radical library give away reading material for free and still fairly compensate the workers making it happen?

• Can booksellers also be bookstore owners? In 2018, the owner of Porter Square Books concocted a plan to sell 49% of his store's ownership interest to a group of longtime employees. I loved this idea so much that I copied it at the Raven—one attempt to make bookselling into a sustainable career.

• Is "indie" even the right move? It's long been a habit to call local, non-chain bookstores "independent bookstores," and I certainly understand that impulse. I address my issues with this term in the introduction, but I also think moving beyond "indie" might allow for the dream of something bigger. What if bookstores aimed for collectivity rather than independence? That could look like collective ownership and the rise of a business model that no longer relies on the wealth of (and generates wealth for) a single person. It could mean increased collectivity among bookstores—the threats outlined in this zine are certainly big enough to warrant more collective action. Of course, it could also mean collective action by booksellers to improve the dignity of their work. Maybe the answer isn't independence but rather interdependence.

CONCLUSION: BUILD A COMMUNITY-ORIENTED, WORKER-FRIENDLY LIFESTYLE

*T*his list can be overwhelming. I fear I get a bit preachy at times. I don't want the main argument for supporting bookstores to be that bookstores are in dire straits. I believe in the work we do and its ability to sustain itself. We provide valuable community and cultural work, and that work can and should make business sense. I believe in a bookstore landscape filled with robust, self-sustaining bookstores that don't have to write zines explaining why they need to be protected and how. But that's not the world we live in, at least not yet. The Republican Party is engaged in a broad and organized effort to repress free speech. Corporate monopolies are shaping our towns and our governments in their image. Greedy executives are driving corporate profits higher and higher even as their companies' workers face stagnating wages and rising costs. Unfortunately, bookstores need protecting, as do American towns and small businesses and workers.

But there's good news: a movement of locally oriented consumers and citizens can take actionable steps to reverse all the above and build a new way of doing things. It's possible to build a world where workers can earn a living wage doing valuable work that doesn't put them at risk. Where people can walk or take a bus to work and shop and eat and play. Where queer kids can see themselves in the books they read without reactionary politicians trying to get in the way. If you've made it to the end of this zine, you have a bunch of strategies to start building that life around you right now.

ABOUT THE AUTHOR

*D*anny Caine is the author of the poetry collections *Continental Breakfast*, *El Dorado Freddy's*, *Flavortown*, and *Picture Window*, as well as the book *How to Resist Amazon and Why*. His poetry has appeared in *The Slowdown*, DIAGRAM, HAD, and *Barrelhouse*, and his prose has appeared in *Literary Hub* and *Publishers Weekly*. In 2019, he received the Midwest Independent Booksellers Association Midwest Bookseller of the Year award. He's a co-owner of the Raven Book Store, *Publishers Weekly's* 2022 bookstore of the year. More at dannycaine.com.

Coming later in 2023

How To Protect BOOKSTORES And Why

THE PRESENT AND FUTURE OF BOOKSELLING

Danny Caine

Author of *How to Resist Amazon and Why*